This book belongs to

_____,

a helpful friend.

Kaydie-Ann Tracey c/o DaGraySky Publications

Ordering Information:
For details, contact admin@dagrayskypublications.org or
dagrayskypublications@gmail.com

English Paperback ISBN: 978-1-0688350-1-8
English eBook ISBN: 978-1-0688350-2-5

Our Climate Action Initiative is to provide an eBook, reducing the need for printed copies.

DEDICATION

This book is lovingly dedicated to my dear parents, whose love and guidance shaped my life beyond measure. Though you are no longer here, your wisdom and kindness continue to inspire me every day.

This story is a **TRIBUTE** to the lessons you taught me about resilience, the courage to face challenges, friendship, and the joy of learning.

I carry your love with me always.

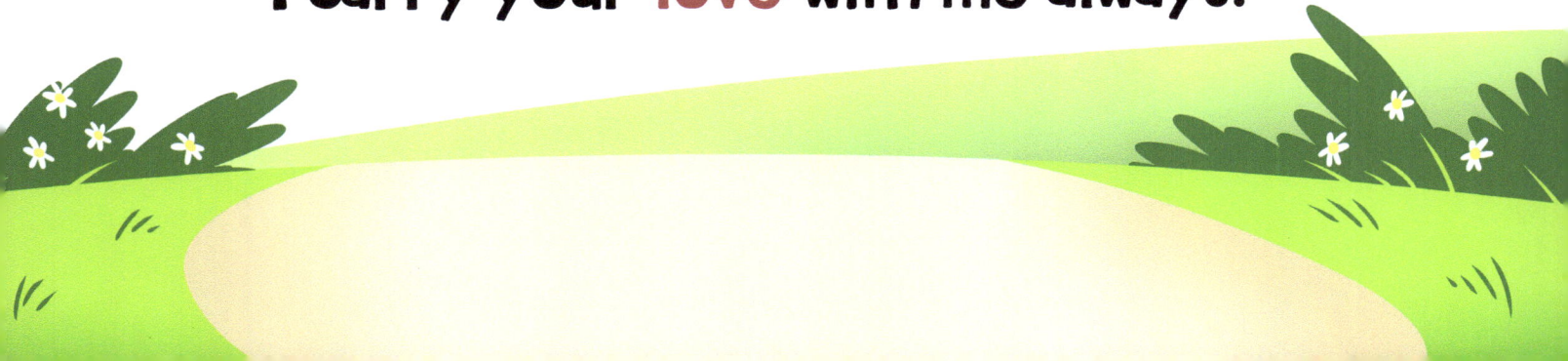

FUN FACT!

Did you know that some people call the game SOCCER and others call it FOOTBALL?

In Canada and a few other places, it's called SOCCER, but in most of the world, including Jamaica where I'm from, it's called FOOTBALL!

No matter what you call it, it's the same exciting game where players kick the ball and try to score goals!

Let's have some fun!

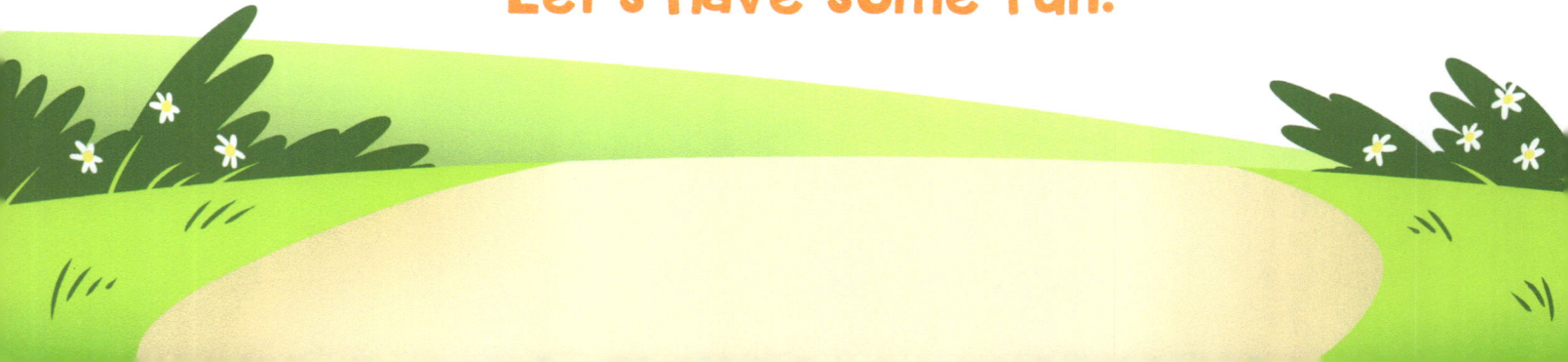

Timmy's Triangle Troubles

By Kaydie-Ann Tracey

Ring, Ring! The recess bell sounded loud and clear. "YEAAAH!" Lunchtime had started, and cheer filled the air.

The long awaited break came at last.

"LOOKOUT!" yelled Timmy the Triangle,

as he blasted past.

Leaping and shouting,

"FOOTBALL, FOOTBALL,

here we come!

It's time to have some fun!"

With his eyes fixed, **no ball** was safe,
Timmy sped across the field, no time to waste.
KICKING the ball with all his might,
it flew over the fence, taking FLIGHT,
completely out of sight.

Timmy was **proud** and **boasted** aloud.

How IMPRESSIVE his kick had been, drew quite the crowd.

However, in the distance, he heard his friends YELLING with great might.

"OH NO, TIMMY! Where's your side?

Don't you see? It's not in sight!"

"Sidney Square, Sidney Square, come and help me! **MY SIDE IS LOST,** no longer a **POLYGON** will I be!"

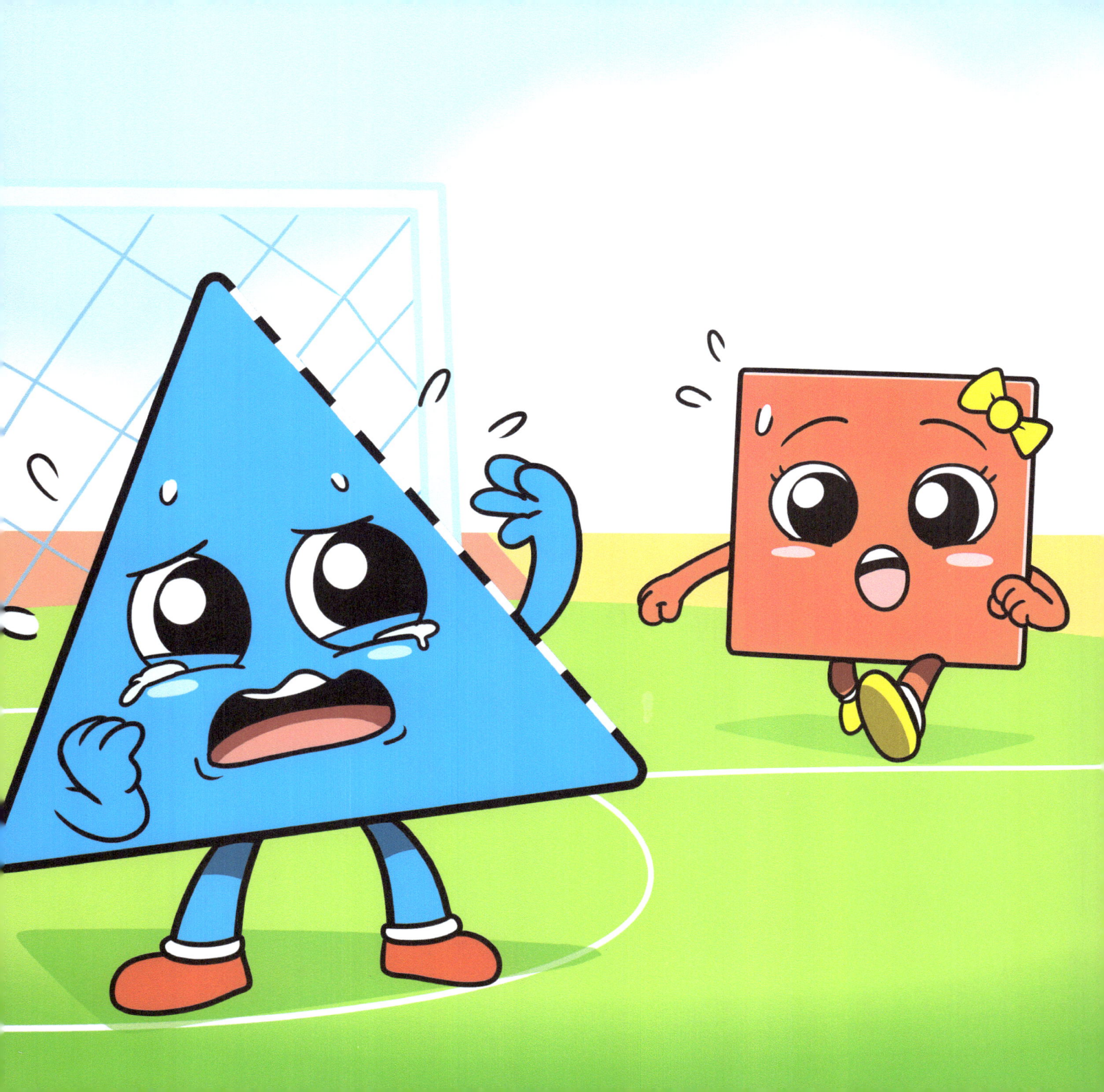

Sidney Square came running as fast as she could.

With all her FOUR SIDES EQUAL

and straight as they should.

"DON'T WORRY Timmy,

we'll find your lost side."

They looked high.

But Timmy's side was nowhere in sight.

"Ricky Rectangle, Ricky Rectangle, come and help me! **MY SIDE IS LOST,** no longer a **POLYGON** will I be!"

Ricky Rectangle came zooming
as fast as he could.

With his **TWO LONG SIDES** and
TWO SHORT SIDES

straight and neat, he looked good.
"DON'T WORRY Timmy,

we will find your lost side."

They looked low.

But Timmy's side was nowhere in sight.

"Sonny Circle, Sonny Circle,
come and help me!
MY SIDE IS LOST,
no longer a **POLYGON** will I be!"

Sonny Circle rolled over, as fast as he could.

"DON'T WORRY Timmy,

we will find your lost side."

They looked far.

But Timmy's side was nowhere in sight.

Just then, Miss Polly Polygon, a teacher so wise,

came to the rescue with a sparkle in her eyes.

"Oh no, you have one angle and two lines,

we won't stop until we've found your lost side.

Let's all take a good look,

we'll SEARCH high, low, far and wide."

The shapes searched, they looked

high, low, **far** and **wide**,

under the slide, and behind the swings, they tried.

Then **Ricky Rectangle** shouted with glee,

"the Sandbox, the Sandbox that's where it'll be!"

PLAYGROUND

Off to the sandbox, side by side,
they reached the sandbox, BIG and WIDE.
Sidney Square found a piece,
so straight and thin,
but it was too short to fit right in!

Ricky Rectangle found a piece too,
long and **tall,**

but it was too big, not right at all.

"**This one's too long,**" Timmy said with a frown,

"my perfect side is nowhere to be found!"

Then **Sonny Circle** came with a piece,
smooth and **round**.
Timmy Triangle frowned, saying,
"that piece is too round!
You won't find that on any **triangle** you see,
all my friends will laugh at me!"

Miss Polly Polygon came with a
PERFECT MATCH.

A **straight, strong side**, no need to patch.

They placed it in, it fit just right,

Timmy Triangle beamed with pure delight!

He was so happy to see,

his missing side safe, as safe as can be!

"One, two, three straight sides,

one, two, three angles,

everyone look, now **I'M A TRIANGLE!"**

Once again a **POLYGON**,

he felt complete.

"THANK YOU my friends for helping me,

that is a problem I don't want to repeat."

So back to the game, they all went to play,

with sides and angles all in the right way.

And **Miss Polly** smiled, with a wink and a cheer,

"SHAPES always stick together,
all throughout the years."

THE END

TIMMY'S HOMEWORK (ACTIVITIES)

WRITING PROMPTS

Creative Writing: "What if you lost one of your sides?
Write what you would do."

_____

_____

_____

_____

Help Timmy:

Timmy lost his side again! Write a letter convincing another shape to come help him.

Include:

- Who the shape is

- Why they should help

- How they'll find the side

- What makes a shape a polygon

_____

_____

_____

_____

Write a short story about how your shape helps Timmy in a new adventure!

_____

_____

_____

_____

_____

_____

_____

_____

COMPREHENSION

Why was Timmy sad?

Ans:_____

Who was the first shape to help him?

Ans:_____

How many sides does a square have?

Ans:_____

WHAT HAPPENED FIRST?

Put the letters in order to show what happened first, next and last in the story:

A. _____ Timmy kicked the football

B. _____ The recess bell rang

C. _____ Timmy ran to the field

ARTS AND CRAFT

Materials: Toothpicks or straws, clay or marshmallows

Instructions: Build Timmy using 3 toothpicks/straws and connectors

Try making:

a. A square (Sidney)

b. A rectangle (Ricky)

c. A circle (can't be made with sticks — Explain why?)

Design a new shape character (e.g., Penny Pentagon)

Draw your own shape for a new character you would add to the story and write their name.

COLOURING AND SHAPE IDENTIFICATION

Colour the scene: Colour the picture of Timmy running on the field. Next, use your imagination to draw and colour where you think the ball went.

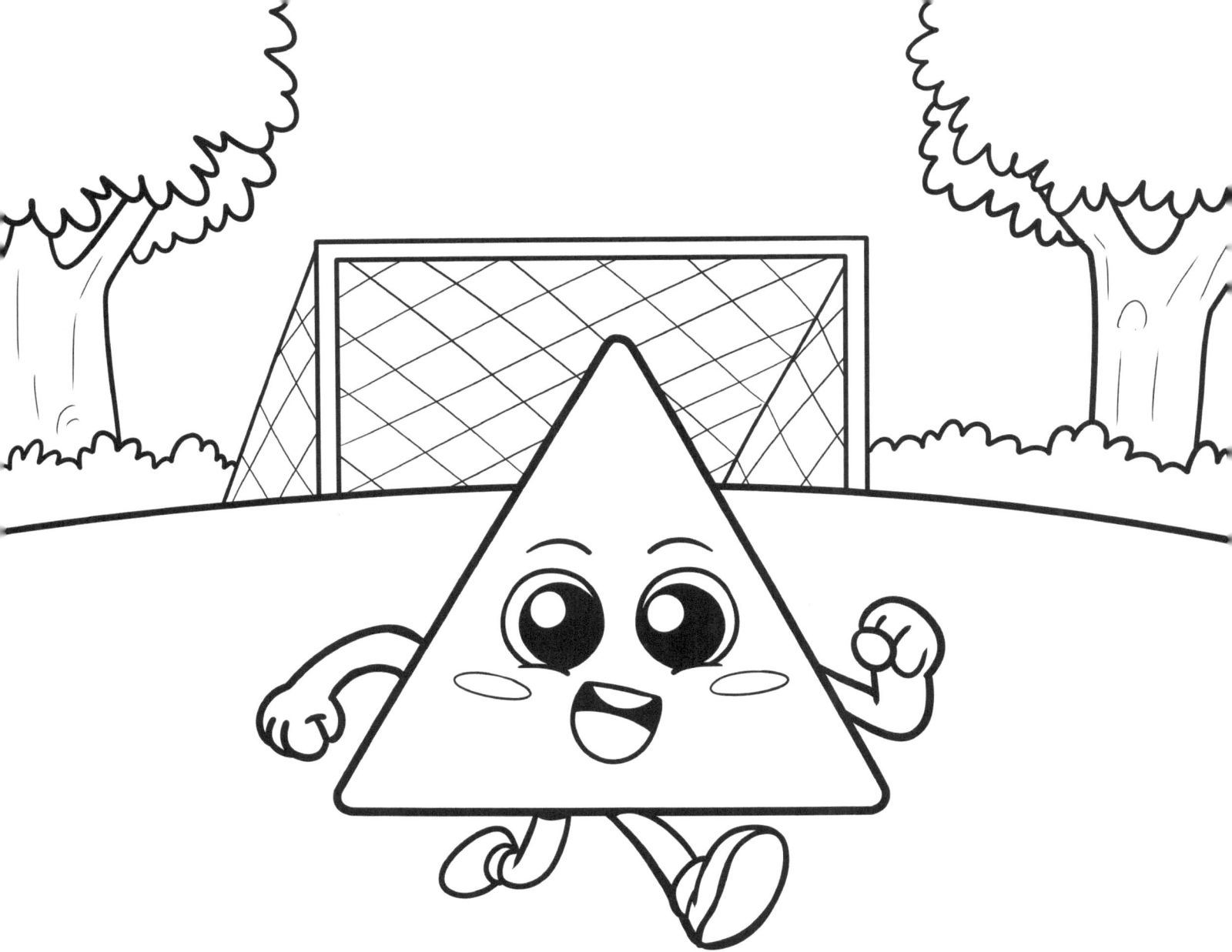

Recognize and name shapes in the picture below,

Materials: Crayons

Colour each shape:

Triangle = Red   Square = Blue

Rectangle = Green   Circle = Yellow

MAZE QUEST

Help Timmy find his way through the maze to his missing side.

MOVEMENT FUN

Lost Side Hunt

Prep: Cut three triangle sides. Then hide one.

Instructions: Child search for missing side (adult hides it)

- Once found, tape/glue the final side to complete Timmy The Triangle.

Active Play

Pretend you are each shape and move like them;

- Triangle: Hop 3 times for 3 sides

- Square: March in a box shape

- Rectangle: Stretch tall, then wide

- Circle: Spin around

Which one was the most fun to move like?

CUT AND MATCH

Instructions: Find and cut out the shapes at the end of the book. Then, read each riddle and match each shape to the right character.

I'm round and roll, no corners to see, I look like a donut or a cookie.

I have three sides, flip me around, I could be a slide.

Four sides are the same, I'm neat and fair, I look like a gift box or a chair

I've got four sides: two short, two long, I'm a Television or a book.

BONUS CHALLENGE:

Look around the room and find real objects that have the same shapes.

Timmy

Sidney

Ricky

Sonny

www.ingramcontent.com/pod-product-compliance
Lightning Source LLC
Chambersburg PA
CBHW060812090426
42737CB00002B/47